Original title:
Hitchhiker's Poetry Guide

Copyright © 2025 Creative Arts Management OÜ
All rights reserved.

Author: Fiona Harrington
ISBN HARDBACK: 978-1-80567-794-9
ISBN PAPERBACK: 978-1-80567-915-8

Navigating the Cosmic Sea

In a galaxy far, so very wide,
Frogs dressed as aliens take us for a ride.
With towels in hand, they laugh and they sing,
On spaceships of jelly, we dance and we fling.

Unicorns pilot, with donuts for wheels,
While rubber duckies show us the feels.
Stars are just confetti, in this cosmic ball,
And we munch on stardust; it tastes like a thrall.

Asteroids spinning like plates on a stick,
A cosmic circus with Martians so slick.
Laughter erupts as we twirl through the night,
Chasing our dreams on a comet's delight.

Through wormholes and rainbows, we frolic and dash,
In a universe where gummy bears splash.
Every moment's a giggle, a wink, or a grin,
As we sail through this whimsy, let the fun begin!

Metaphysical Musings on the Road to Forever

On a road paved with weirdness, we set off our quest,
With a toasty toaster as our sage and our guest.
Spouting wisdom with every toasted slice,
It tells us that the journey's the real paradise.

With socks on our heads and hats on our feet,
We argue with penguins over something to eat.
Infinite ice cream, flavors galore,
A parade of marshmallows, who could ask for more?

Quantum ducks wish us luck with a quack,
Flying in circles, then headin' right back.
They say the key's laughter, to float past the stars,
While eating moon pies, and racing cool cars.

Time ticks like a chicken, so silly and bright,
Spinning through moments, oh what a delight!
The road stretches onward, ever twisting and turning,
In the heart of forever, it's all about yearning!

Verses that Cross Boundaries.

On a cosmic bus, aliens sing,
With doughnuts flying on a string.
A three-headed dog fetches stars,
While Earthlings giggle in funky cars.

Wormholes twist like pretzel dreams,
Galactic cafes serve whipped cream beams.
Space cows moo in wobbly tunes,
As stardust dances with cartoon loons.

Galactic Journeys Unbound.

Riding rockets made of cheese,
Traveling far, just with a sneeze.
Jellybeans guide our flashy route,
While giggling meteors give a toot.

A wise old robot gives us tips,
Sips of plasma with potato chips.
Together we laugh at cosmic pranks,
As we float through the Milky Flanks.

Cosmic Verses on the Wind.

Planets waltz on a galactic line,
With cosmic dust that tastes like brine.
Silly space pirates in pajama hats,
Trade in laughter, not gold or mats.

A spaceship sails on candy canes,
While crazy comets play silly games.
Stars wear sunglasses, taking a dip,
In cosmic pools, they do a flip.

The Interstellar Travelogues.

In the void where giggles reside,
Quantum jokers take a ride.
Snapping fingers makes stars appear,
Confetti bursts in zeroes, dear.

With rubber planets and bouncy moons,
We sing along with silly tunes.
A rhyming comet whistles a score,
As we dance with the universe, wanting more.

The Road Less Traveled—In Rhyme

With a thumb up high, I stand in wait,
A ride will come, oh, isn't fate great?
Each driver tells tales, bizarre and wild,
With laughter and snacks, I feel like a child.

From cows in the back to cats in the front,
Every journey's a story, a whimsical stunt.
Road signs twist words in a playful dance,
Life's a funride, so take a chance!

Whispers from the Abyss

I asked the void for a sidekick's lore,
It chuckled back, 'I've seen it before!'
With cosmic giggles and stardust cheer,
The abyss shelves tales that tickle the ear.

Galactic pirates and asteroids fly,
Caffeine-fueled comets zooming on by.
In the dark, there's a joke, it's really quite clear,
Space is just weird, let's grab a cold beer!

The Hitchhiker's Lament

My ride's running late, I huff and I puff,
The thumb gets tired; this waiting is tough.
But a zany old chap with a parrot in tow,
Said, 'Don't fret my friend, just go with the flow!'

With tales of odd lands and existential dread,
He spun yarns of worlds where toasters are fed.
I laughed at the weirdness, the absurdity bright,
A lament turned to joy, under stars of the night!

Beyond the Speed of Light

Zooming through space in a ship made of dreams,
Time makes no sense; it's not what it seems.
A scenic detour past planets of cheese,
Gargling green aliens wave as they sneeze.

At warp speed we go, with some snacks on the side,
Laughing at physics, and taking in stride.
As light bends and dances, we giggle and cheer,
The universe is silly, let's boogie, my dear!

In Search of Infinite Lines

I asked the stars for guidance,
They winked and rolled their eyes.
A comet sneezed and traveled far,
Left behind a trail of fries.

A spaceship waved, a friendly sight,
It honked and then it spun.
"Join me for a cosmic ride!"
"We might just find some fun!"

I packed my bag, I packed my hat,
And searched for knickknack gold.
With all the universe to roam,
I aimed for dreams untold.

But in this vast, uncharted sprawl,
I lost my way to dine.
The guidebook flipped; I found myself
In line for alien wine.

Echoes of the Cosmic Road

What's that sound, a rumbling star?
A beat from Mars, perhaps?
An alien band, they drive me wild,
While I twist my spacey laps.

A plaid-wearing Martian plays the flute,
While asteroids jump and groove.
I danced so hard I lost a shoe,
But hey, I've found my move!

Galactic giggles echo loud,
Those laughter beams collide.
With every chuckle, time expands,
And I'm along for the ride.

The road is filled with cosmic jokes,
As planets line up for fries.
Every mile a punchline waits,
Underneath the endless skies.

The Randomness of Celestial Hitching

There's a bus stop on a starry spree,
With seats made out of dreams.
I sit beside a purple whale,
And sip my cosmic creams.

A spaceship stops, all shiny bright,
The driver grins with glee.
"Hop aboard, we're off to Pluto!
Or maybe just a tree!"

The randomness keeps piling up,
As satellites twist and twirl.
An octopus plays poker there,
While I give space a whirl.

Through wormholes and bizarre routes,
The laughter never ends.
With every hitch, I learn to laugh,
Making spacey, silly friends.

Starlit Highways

Oh, the highways of the night,
   Twinkling with intent.
I cruise in my bizarre old ship,
   With snacks of every scent.

Galaxies zoom in bumper-to-bumper,
   They're stuck in cosmic jam.
I pass by laughing cosmic cows,
   While munching moonlit ham.

The starlit signs point every way,
   Some even upside down.
My GPS just sings in rhyme,
   And tells me, "Don't you frown!"

Who knew that space could be so fun?
   With every twist and turn.
I'll hitch a ride through cosmic lanes,
   And let my laughter burn.

The Luminary Chronicles

In a spaceship made of cheese,
A mouse piloted with ease,
Through cosmic dust and playful quirks,
Avoiding aliens in their perks.

With stars for hats and moons for shoes,
They danced in colors, pink and blues.
Galactic giggles filled the air,
As planets watched from everywhere.

Chasing comets, racing light,
Fueling laughter, what a sight!
In the void, where silence dwells,
They sang of fish and wishing wells.

Finally landing on a star,
They toasted life from near and far.
With every wink, a story spun,
In the glow of the cosmic fun.

Routines of the Relentless Wanderer

Breakfast on a floating cloud,
With syrup made from starlight proud.
A space fork and a gravity plate,
Eating breakfast—oh, it's great!

Wandering worlds with silly names,
Playing interstellar games.
Twirling with a Saturn ring,
Living life like a cosmic king.

Yet every night, the same old plots,
Finding socks among the knots.
Theories on how to snore in space,
Making friends at a slow pace.

Each planet, a stop to explore,
Charming aliens with tales galore.
Though routines may seem a bit nuts,
They add spice to the cosmic cuts.

When Poetry Meets the Cosmos

Ode to the nebulae bright,
With colors swirling in the night.
A sonnet sung by a galaxy wide,
Whispering secrets where dreams collide.

Limericks bounce off meteor trails,
Sailing through spaces where humor prevails.
Jokes from quasars, puns in the dust,
All thrown in a spaceship, it's a must!

Haikus drift in the solar wind,
Crafted by stars, whimsily pinned.
Rhymes that dance like the Milky Way,
Tickling comets to brighten the day.

In the void where echoes play,
Words float freely, come what may.
When poetry stumbles, and stars laugh anew,
We discover the cosmos—through and through.

Wonders of the Celestial Voyage

Through stardust, our travelers glide,
On moons where jellybeans reside.
Aliens join in a lively spree,
Sipping stardust tea, fancy and free.

They skip on rings with gumdrop glee,
Playing tag with a curious bee.
Jupiter's storms become their game,
As laughter echoes, never the same.

With each whirl, a tale unfolds,
Cosmic treasures and secrets bold.
Navigating a universe so wide,
Each wanderer, a joyful guide.

When all is done, they'll trace their route,
Finding joy in the cosmic scout.
For wonders abound in the night so grand,
In a universe that's perfectly planned.

Journeys Beyond the Known

In a ship made of cheese, we sail the stars,
Dodging space cows and flying cars.
With each twist and turn, we break the mold,
Adventures jolly, in stories untold.

Through cosmic bars we order a drink,
With Martians who teach us to think.
A toast to the odd, let's raise a cheer,
For laughter echoes, year after year.

Poetic Thumbs in the Void

A thumb outstretched in the galactic night,
Waiting for rides from creatures of light.
With toes in a twist, and giggles galore,
We hitch a lift on a comet's roar.

Bouncing on beams, laughing in glee,
A penguin drives past, just look and see!
With a wink and a nod, the stars do play,
In a universe where odd's the new gay.

The Universe on a Thumbprint

Each thumbprint's a world, so vast, so wide,
Where jelly beans dance with nowhere to hide.
From moons made of marshmallows, sticky and sweet,
To suns that can giggle and glide on their feet.

If we roll with the punches, we might just catch,
A ride from a floaty, a giddy match.
Among galaxies swirling, we'll paint the sky,
With laughter and chaos, oh my, oh my!

Vagabond Verses

On a whim we wander, no map in sight,
Finding joy in the awkward, the silly delight.
With a wink to the stars, we dance on the breeze,
Vagabonds of verse, doing just as we please.

With verses that tumble like dice in a game,
Insisting that all absurdity's tame.
So join in the fun, let's make some noise,
In the chaos of space, we discover our joys.

Chronicles of the Comet's Tail

A comet zips by with a wink,
It teases the stars, what do they think?
In the tail, a party is brewing,
With aliens dancing and cosmic brewing.

Close your eyes, let the stardust rain,
Floating in space, forget all the pain.
Galactic giggles echo and swell,
Oh, what a ride! It's a tale to tell.

Songs of the Celestial Highway

On the cosmic road, we take our chance,
Hitching a ride, join the galactic dance.
Traffic jams of meteors and stars,
Blast off together, forget the cars.

With friendly voices on the radio,
Singing of planets, where wishes flow.
Navigating winks from Venus tonight,
Laughing at black holes, what a delight!

An Astronomer's Heartfelt Lines

A telescope's eye can see so far,
But who needs that when you are a star?
Coffee brewed strong, with a sprinkle of dreams,
Charting the skies, or so it seems.

Counting the satellites drifting by,
Each one a wish that I can't deny.
Each twinkling dot holds a giggle tight,
In this cosmic riddle, all feels so right.

Tales from the Seat of a Starship

Strapped in tight in my shiny ship,
With a cup of tea, I take a zip.
Warp speed ahead with a snicker and cheer,
Floating through space with naught but good beer.

Galactic bar hop, stars floating near,
Laughing with aliens, sharing a beer.
Stories get taller, as we laugh and sigh,
In this grand journey, we're all gung-ho, bye!

Echoes of the Universe in Motion

In the vastness where stars collide,
A sock lost in space, a cosmic ride.
Galactic giggles echo afar,
As planets dance around a funny star.

Asteroids roll like bowling balls,
While comets make whimsical calls.
Space cats chase the celestial mice,
In the void, there's always something nice.

With each burst of laughter, light unfolds,
Tales of travelers, their mischief told.
Nebulas swirl in a rainbow hue,
Where space and humor deftly brew.

Amongst the chaos and interstellar jam,
A tiny spaceship's out for a scam.
Twinkling giggles from Venus to Mars,
The universe sings beneath the stars.

Stanzas in the Spaces Between

In the silence where the cosmos hums,
Jokes ripple out like asteroid drums.
Wormholes wink with a playful grin,
In the fabric of space, laughter begins.

A comet hiccups, trailing its tail,
While wise old moons tell outrageous tales.
Galaxies spin with a jolly twist,
In the void, how could you resist?

Quasars belch in a cosmic burp,
Creating art with a cosmic slurp.
Time travelers chuckle, sipping tea,
In the paradox of eternity.

So float along this merry route,
Where nonsense and laughter play out.
In the stardust, funny stories dwell,
In the spaces between, they weave their spell.

A Traveler's Rhapsody Through Time

With time pods zooming through the fray,
Past the days of yore and yesterday.
The jester of ages, cap and bell,
Rides the currents where the past can dwell.

Dinosaurs chuckle at the latest styles,
While knights joust with absurd, silly smiles.
In the Renaissance, paint drips and quips,
From the brush of a jester with witty scripts.

Round and round in a timey wimey way,
Curly wigs and spandex in bright display.
Poking fun at history's grand parade,
Oh, the tales of giggles time has made!

So hop on board this comical ride,
Where moments tickle as they glide.
Every second is a chance to jest,
In the chronicles of time's grand fest.

The Written Stars Above

Beneath the stars, where stories bloom,
Each twinkle whispers tales of gloom.
But wait! A chuckle from a planet near,
Turns solemn vibes into laughter's cheer.

Written in stardust, jokes entwine,
While meteors drop with a funny line.
Cosmic comedians light up the night,
With punchlines flying, oh what a sight!

Galaxies giggle, constellations tease,
The universe spins with the greatest ease.
A celestial script, penned in delight,
Painting the cosmos in warmth so bright.

So look above at the cosmic show,
With each shooting star, let laughter flow.
The written stars tell of fun ahead,
In the sky, where dreams are fed.

Fables of the Faraway

In a galaxy not so far,
A green man danced with a star.
He lost his shoe in a black hole,
But laughed it off, that silly soul.

With a towel on his head so bold,
He bartered secrets for some gold.
A cosmic market, strange and bright,
Where fish could sing and rocks took flight.

He met a cat who spoke in rhymes,
Telling tales of lost good times.
They shared a laugh, a cosmic cheer,
And left behind their earthly fear.

So when you wander far and wide,
Remember joy is your best guide.
In every star, in every space,
There's fun to find in this vast place.

Poems for the Cosmic Drifter

A roguish comet rides the breeze,
Tickling planets, shaking trees.
It hosts a party, wild and free,
Where even asteroids sip tea.

There's laughter echoing in the void,
A quirky world where time's destroyed.
The aliens play hopscotch with light,
While squids debate the colors bright.

With a wink from a sunbeam's flare,
A traveler finds they have no care.
For in this place where oddities bloom,
A smile can chase away the gloom.

So toss your worries to the stars,
Join in the dance, forget your scars.
The universe is one big joke,
Just laugh along and take a poke.

A Traveler's Melancholy

A spaceship's lost its way again,
Its pilot's stuck in memory's pen.
He ponders stars that used to shine,
While sipping tea from a plastic vine.

Through nebulae of muted hues,
He hums a tune of cosmic blues.
With every hiccup, time does sway,
Where yesterday feels far away.

Yet in the drift, a spark ignites,
A ghostly laugh at odd delights.
He spots a comet wearing shades,
And chuckles at its silly masquerades.

So let your heart roam freely, friend,
In every twist, there's joy to lend.
For every sigh in solitude,
Brings laughter in the interlude.

Musings Under an Alien Sky

Beneath a sky of jelly beans,
An octopus juggles with machines.
It tells the universe a joke,
While friendly lightning bugs all poke.

The stars are giggling, twinkling bright,
As rocket ships take off in flight.
If you listen closely, you'll hear,
A cosmic giggle drawing near.

Wormholes twist in a playful spin,
Where all the chaos feels like kin.
A paradox in every rhyme,
Making sense in the silliest time.

So gather round, both brave and shy,
Under this wacko alien sky.
The fun's contagious, come and play,
In the cosmos, laughter leads the way.

Celestial Musings and Cosmic Rhymes

In a galaxy far and wide,
The stars giggle, they won't hide.
Planets dance in cosmic glee,
Winking at you, oh can't you see?

Spaceships made of cheese and bread,
Aliens joke in every thread.
A comet's tail, a flaky grin,
Even black holes swallow sin.

Nebulas paint with splashes bright,
While lightyears pass in pure delight.
Asteroids roll, a cosmic game,
Universal fun, it's never tame.

Galactic laughter fills the void,
Every mystery just enjoyed.
So float with joy on starlit seas,
Where gags outshine the milky breeze.

Poems for the Galactic Wayfarer

With puns as fuel, we take to flight,
Across the void, oh what a sight!
Quasars beam a gleeful tune,
As we orbit bright, mischievous moon.

Astrobiologists in a stew,
Guess the taste of Martian stew.
Zany trips on Saturn's rings,
Sharing stories of strange things.

Asteroids wearing silly hats,
Joking about the weight of cats.
Warp speed laughing all the way,
Comics written in stardust play.

So take a ride, embrace the jest,
In this cosmic quest, be your best.
Every planet a stage to roam,
In the universe, we find our home.

A Journey Written in the Stars

Wish upon a comet's tail,
For a tale that's bound to sail.
Galaxies whisper, giggling bright,
Painting dreams in the nightlight.

A starship made of dreams and fun,
Traveling where the stories run.
Planets share their wildest schemes,
Beneath the glow of cosmic beams.

Shooting stars and cosmic fries,
Laughter rolls across the skies.
Every asteroid's a playground fair,
Where joy is found in every glare.

So wander far and wander wide,
With jokes as company, be your guide.
In stellar realms of mirth and cheer,
The universe holds laughter dear.

Luminous Lines from the Last Frontier

Light-years stretch, they twist and curl,
In this vast and wacky whirl.
Jokes float like cosmic dust,
In starlit laughter, wanderlust.

Nebulas swirl in joyful spins,
Making fun of all our sins.
While supernovas burst in jest,
They light the way, we feel so blessed.

Aliens crack jokes in the void,
While humans ponder, oft annoyed.
Yet in this dance of cosmic play,
Find joy in every silly sway.

So gather round, the stars align,
In this endless joke divine.
With Luminous lines, we'll take our share,
Laughing out loud, everywhere!

Verses for the Stardust Seeker

In the cosmos, I roam and spin,
With a towel wrapped tight, I take it all in.
Stars giggle softly, they twinkle and tease,
While planets play tag, and asteroids flee.

Floating through space with a cheerful grin,
Chasing comets, where to begin?
A banana-shaped ship, it veers and sways,
Who knew the Milky Way could dance in such ways?

With cosmic candy in pockets I find,
The universe chuckles, oh so unkind.
But here with my pals, in this stellar parade,
Every strange quirk is a heavenly trade.

So grab me a star, let's see what it costs,
Even if we trip over black holes and lost.
The travels are wild, the laughter's the key,
In the stardust we seek, we'll always be free.

Narrative Threads in the Dark Matter

In the void where the whispers of cosmos collide,
I spun a few tales where the dark things reside.
A sock lost to time with a mysterious fate,
It danced with a photon and flirted with fate.

My friend, the odd quark, told stories of woe,
Of particles misplacing their masks in a show.
The vacuum chuckled, a storybook vast,
As neutrinos giggled, darting too fast.

With laughter like light, we wove our great tales,
Of gravity's mischief and interstellar gales.
A paradox here and a pun over there,
In the theater of matter, there's joy everywhere.

So gather your thoughts, let them drift through the void,
In dark matter, plots and plans are deployed.
Each narrative dust, like stars in a swirl,
Is a piece of our laughter, in this whimsical world.

Ephemeral Dreams in Zero Gravity

In zero gravity, we tumble and float,
Chasing odd dreams in a curious boat.
I dreamt of a sandwich that flew like a kite,
It whizzed past the stars, oh what a sight!

The moon winks at me, a cheeky old friend,
As jellybeans orbit, my snacks on the mend.
The sun beams in laughter, a playful chase,
While I spin and twirl in this weightless space.

With rainbows of jelly and stardust for cake,
We fumble our wishes, for laughter's own sake.
In laughter's embrace, not a worry in view,
We dance through the cosmos with dreams made anew!

So grab a spoonful of cosmic delight,
In the fabric of dreams, let's dance through the night.
Each giggle's a rocket to the farthest of skies,
Where wishes are made and the laughter never dies.

The Lost Verses of the Universe

In corners unseen, where the galaxies hum,
Lie verses forgotten, awaiting some fun.
I found a lost phrase wrapped tight in some dust,
It giggled with glee, for it knew it was just.

With time slipping by, I sketched out a rhyme,
That shimmered with stardust, so quirky, sublime.
It whispered of planets, of wild cosmic spins,
And the secrets of black holes where adventure begins.

Each line an endeavor, a burst of pure joy,
Surprising as comets, like a child with a toy.
We chuckled at echoes of forgotten pursuits,
The universe chuckling in colorful suits!

So come join the quest for these lyrical gems,
In the cosmos of whims, we'll craft rhymes and phlegms.
For laughter is stardust, a mix of delight,
In the lost verses found, we'll dance through the night.

Beyond Infinity: A Poetic Quest

In a galaxy of socks, they roam,
Fleeting thoughts, like bees, call home.
With pens that scribble and laugh aloud,
They dance on words, a happy crowd.

Amidst the stars, a cat once dreamed,
Of rainbow fish and ice cream streams.
In cosmic highways, they take a ride,
With jokes and verses, side by side.

Their spaceship's fueled by tea and glee,
With every laugh, they're wild and free.
Under moons that wobble, they debate,
What's larger: the sky, or a dinner plate?

So join the quest, don't lose the chance,
To write with giggles, to leap, to dance.
In the absurdity of space, take your aim,
For serious poets, it's not a game.

Drifting Words in the Void

Words float like balloons in the dark,
Chasing stars while sharing a spark.
Each letter hops from one to another,
Dancing around like a jolly blubber.

In the silence, rhymes burst loud,
Silly phrases, they wear like a shroud.
With a chuckle here and a silly pun there,
They drift through cosmos, free and rare.

Gravitation can't hold them tight,
As they giggle through the endless night.
With meteors made of paper and ink,
They scribble their dreams without a wink.

So grab a line and hold it close,
In this quirky void, we all can boast.
For in drifting words, we find our art,
A universe crafted from the heart.

The Lost Stanzas of Universe

Somewhere, lost in cosmic flows,
Stanzas whisper, tickling toes.
They mingle with comets, oh so bright,
Spinning tales through the endless night.

An astronaut stumbles, not on the moon,
But on verses that make him croon.
With every rhyme, he juggles his fate,
In this lost cosmos, it's never too late.

Galaxies giggle at outdated prose,
As new rhymes blossom, like blooming a rose.
With laughter echoing past planetary halls,
The lost stanzas answer the call.

So pen your verse with a wink and a nod,
In this quirky realm, we've all been trod.
With every word that twirls and sways,
We uncover the universe in playful ways.

Verses for the Wayward Traveler

Oh traveler caught in a cosmic spree,
Chasing dreams near a green-eyed tree.
With wishes tucked inside a backpack,
And plans that seem to always lack.

You've danced with time, with a spoon and fork,
And met a duck that could really talk.
Together you rode on a passing cloud,
Crafting tales that'd make you proud.

Your path is wild, like a winding road,
Each step a punchline, laughter bestowed.
With every stumble, a rhyme appears,
To echo through space for countless years.

So wander on, dear poet at heart,
In realms where silly and profound depart.
For every verse, whether lost or found,
Is a treasure chest with joy unbound.

Celestial Thumbs Up

Thumbs up to the cosmos bright,
With aliens dancing in the light.
They wave with toes and twirl with flair,
While I just stand and gawk and stare.

Each comet trails a silly grin,
As starships zoom and zoom back in.
I think they know a joke or two,
But I forgot my interstellar cue.

From Mars, they send me strange requests,
Like 'Bring us snacks, but not the rest!'
I laugh and think, 'Oh, what a sight!'
These cosmic pals are pure delight.

So hitch a ride on this wild spree,
With cosmic pals and laughter free.
In galaxies far, we'll make a scene,
And write our tales of in-betweens.

Starlit Scribbles

Under starlit skies, we scribble dreams,
With meteor showers bursting at the seams.
A quokka in space, what a funny thought,
Sketching with pencils we just bought.

Jupiter jumps, Saturn swings wide,
As we doodle on our crazy ride.
Each scribble tells a comical tale,
Of penguins in rocket ships, they set sail.

A unicorn rides on a cosmic wave,
With giggling fairies, oh, how they crave.
The ink flows free, like a shooting star,
As we craft our visions, near and far.

What's that? A spaceship? No, just a kite,
Flapping in laughter, oh what a sight!
Our canvas stretches from here to zen,
In this playful universe, we'll fly again.

Verses from the Edge of the Universe

At the edge of space, where lost socks roam,
I penned down verses, far from home.
With black holes chuckling as they suck,
I found the words, oh what luck!

Aliens chime in with witty rhymes,
Spinning tales of old lost times.
They giggle at our earthly trends,
And lend advice 'to make amends.'

Gravity grins, makes me trip and fall,
While cosmic winds seem to call.
At this fringe, where time unwinds,
Laughter echoes through the cosmic blinds.

So here's a toast to the stars above,
To laughter shared and a little love.
From the edge where realities merge,
We pen our verses, our fates converge.

The Wayfarer's Lament

The road is long, the stars poorly mapped,
With every hitch, my patience tapped.
In cosmic cabs, I sit and wait,
As time wobbles on, all too late.

An octopus driver, quite the sight,
Says he's lost, gets the exit right.
With eight arms waving, it's a wild ride,
Through swirling galaxies, we glide!

Where's my towel? Did I leave it back?
In wormholes, yes, it vanished, whack!
Each stop's a giggle, each bump a cheer,
In the wayfarer's world, there's nothing to fear!

So I'll laugh at each twist and turn we take,
Embrace the chaos, for joy's at stake.
In cosmic travels, we find our groove,
And in this dance, our spirits move!

Rhymes of the Unseen Road

I thumb my way through cosmic lanes,
Dodging aliens and silly trains.
My thumb says yes, the stars agree,
While space cows moo in harmony.

Galactic hitch, a joyful mess,
With every ride, I must confess,
A funny tale unfolds in flight,
As comets giggle through the night.

Planets wink as we swirl and twirl,
I'd trade my snacks for intergalactic pearl.
And if I get a lift from Mars,
I'll never need to count the stars!

So here's a tip, ye riders bold,
Always carry snacks when stories unfold.
For every cosmic ride we take,
The punchlines land in every shake.

Poems from the Backseat of Time

In the backseat of a car so wide,
I scribble rhymes on time's great ride.
With seatbelts fastened, laughter flies,
As time loops round with silly sighs.

I peek through windows at the past,
Where dinosaurs dance and gnomes run fast.
The driver says, "Buckle tight,
It's a bumpy road to future sight!"

A detour leads to moments grand,
Where history's written in chicken hand.
We sip on jokes from cups of glee,
In this fast track of giddy spree.

So let's rewind, fast-forward too,
Creating fun from moments new.
For every mile we laugh and rhyme,
The journey's worth in quirky time.

Stanzas Between Dimensions

Between the worlds, we spin and sway,
With dimensions dancing in a funny way.
A cat plays chess with an alien king,
While nonchalance trails from every fling.

I travel through doors that twist and grin,
Where shadows play at every spin.
And in the corner, there's a door labeled 'fun,'
I feel the universe wink at the pun!

The fabric of space is a patchwork quilt,
Stitched with giggles and dreams we built.
I poke at stars with my cosmic pen,
As they scribble back, "Let's do it again!"

So let's toast to the laughter we find,
In the stanzas where space is unlined.
Each jump we take might be absurd,
Yet joy is contained in every word.

The Road Less Written

On a path where stories twist and turn,
Adventures call, and futures burn.
A road sign reads, 'Choose your whim,'
Where jokes take flight and logic swims.

I met a snail that danced in place,
With rhythms set to outer space.
He said, "Just follow me, my friend,
In laughter, all roads will blend!"

Through whimsical woods of wordy plots,
I strolled with aliens and oversized knots.
Each step I took in joy was clear,
As every step drew laughter near.

So write your tale on this spirited lane,
For the road less written is never a pain.
In joy and fun, every bump and skip,
Turns life's journey to a wild trip.

Starlit Stanzas in Transit

In a galaxy wide, full of folk,
A three-headed beast just told a joke.
The stars winked back, bright and plush,
While comets raced by with a loud, silly rush.

In spaceships of candy, they zoom and they glide,
With interstellar snacks, a feast to provide.
One green alien danced, all out of tune,
While the moon chuckled softly, a shimmering boon.

With rings made of bubbles, they twirl and they spin,
Planetary parades, they're ready to win.
Asteroids giggle, they can't help but sway,
As cosmic music plays on this fine day.

So bring your odd hats and shoes made of cheese,
Join this mad dance, let laughter appease.
With friends from afar, let's share in the glee,
In starlit stanzas, forever we'll be.

Poems from Beyond the Milky Way

A quirky creature with seven big eyes,
Scribbles his verses 'neath violet skies.
His tales of bizarre, outlandish delight,
Left everyone giggling, even the night.

In starships with wheels, they zoom past the sun,
With knickknacks and knickknacks, they're having such fun.
A chorus of chuckles in the vacuum of space,
Warping through humor, at a ludicrous pace.

The moons all agree, it's a riotous fest,
With planets and asteroids joining the jest.
As meteors sing and do a little jig,
We laugh through the cosmos, oh so big!

So let this be known, from Andromeda's edge,
That laughter's a treasure, a universal pledge.
In poems from realms where the wild spirits play,
We find all the smiles hidden far away.

Messages in a Bottle of Stardust

In bottles of stardust, they send little notes,
From wormholes and worlds, full of improbable quotes.
A fishbowl of nebulae, swirling around,
Holds secrets of humor, waiting to be found.

With laughter as currency, they trade and they share,
A giggle for a snack, or an old rubber bear.
Each letter a riddle, each word like a game,
In the vast, silly void, they're wild and untame.

They craft crazy wishes on shooting stars,
Using glittery constellations as bars.
With their jokes packed in crates, launching wide-eyed,
Messages float under the universe's tide.

So open your heart, let the laughter leak,
For joy of the cosmos is oh so unique.
In bottles of stardust, let whimsy take flight,
With messages wrapped in the soft glow of night.

Rhyme Between the Stars

In the bounce and the boing of a rogue astral leap,
Rhyme danced with rhythm, no need for sleep.
Galactic giggles ricochet through the void,
As silly old time-warping pranks are deployed.

Planetary rhymes twirl like paper planes,
In a cosmic bazaar where the absurd entertains.
Whirling with joy, as gravity bends,
The punchlines are crackling, oh what fun it sends!

Each quasar a joker, with a twinkle and grin,
Poking fun at the starlight, just wanting to spin.
With laughter like comets, they trail through the night,
Illuminating dreams, oh what a sight!

So gather your friends from across the expanse,
Join the rhyme in the stars for a whimsical dance.
In the universe vast, where silliness gleams,
We'll rhyme through the cosmos, chasing our dreams.

Wanderlust Verses

In a café on the moon, I sipped some brew,
A talking cat asked where I wandered to.
I said, 'Just here for fish and some fun,'
He winked, replied, 'Take the rocket, run!'

On Neptune, I danced with a polka-dot squid,
He wore a top hat; quite the fancy kid.
Together we twirled under swirling lights,
As aliens cheered through the starry nights.

At dusk on Mars, we had tacos and pie,
Made by a chef who was also a spy.
He whispered secrets of asteroids bright,
Gave me a map to a comet's flight.

So if you seek laughter, just take the plunge,
Book a trip to the stars, don't hesitate, lunge.
For every mile traveled, you'll find a weird tale,
Adventure awaits in the cosmic snail!

Cosmic Stanzas

A spaceship zoomed by, with a wink and a grin,
Inside was a robot who only made din.
He offered me cupcakes shaped like a star,
Said, 'These sweet bites will take you far!'

Nebula clouds wrapped us in candy floss,
While space whales sang of our next big loss.
'We'll find a planet where grass is blue,'
They bubbled with laughter, 'And no one feels blue!'

In an asteroid belt, we played hide and seek,
Dodging asteroids that were quite unique.
One yelled, 'You found me!' as it rolled on by,
I chuckled and waved at the passing sky.

So come join the fun in the great unknown,
With laughter and joy, we'll never be alone.
Through cosmic stanzas, let's frolic and spin,
Adventure awaits; let the madness begin!

Traveler's Rhyme

With a wink and a smile, I hitched a ride,
On a comet's tail, zooming side to side.
The driver was llamas in sunglasses cool,
They said, 'Buckle up; we're no ordinary fools!'

The stars looked down and giggled with glee,
As we danced in zero gravity, just me.
One llama declared, 'Let's find a new place,
Where gravity's light, and we all can race!'

A planet of marshmallows came into view,
We bounced and we ate, just two of the crew.
They offered me s'mores made of pure light,
As we laughed through the cosmos, hearts feeling bright.

So strap on your boots, keep your eyes open wide,
Adventure ahead, let your issues subside.
In this traveler's rhyme, we'll make silly noise,
With laughter and joy, let's all be the toys!

Galactic Journey's Ode

In a rocket fueled by chocolate and cheer,
I soared through the cosmos with nothing to fear.
My co-pilot, a squirrel with a bright red cape,
Together we plotted our next big escape.

We landed on a world where time ran slow,
Hopping on clouds made of jelly-like dough.
Local beings had horns and wiggly tails,
They joined our dance; laughter echoed in gales.

I traded my hat for a glowing green gift,
A map made of stardust, a cosmic lift.
Off to find treasures not seen by the eye,
Where wishes are planted and dreams get to fly.

So gather your friends, put your worries on hold,
In this galactic ode, let the adventures unfold.
For every journey is filled with pure glee,
Just look for the joy, and you'll always be free!

Footsteps on Alien Moons

In purple grass, we dance and twirl,
Spinning tales in an alien whirl.
A three-eyed dog just stole my hat,
Now I'm stuck in a conversation with that!

Sipping soup from a floating cup,
Levitating spoons, oh, what a setup!
My feet are stuck in gooey glue,
At least the stars are bright and true.

Conversations with a talking rock,
It says I'm late for a cosmic clock.
I chuckle, though I know it's wrong,
Because time here is just a silly song.

When shadows stretch, and the night is deep,
I ride a comet, oh how sweet!
With aliens laughing and no care,
I've lost my way, but who would dare?

Across the Cosmos with a Quill

I wrote a letter to a star,
It answered back from afar.
In ink made from stardust bright,
It caught my thoughts in pure delight.

The quill, it flies like a spaceship gleam,
Crafting rhymes, a cosmic dream.
Each word I pen, a universe spun,
With giggles shared and laughter run.

I warned a black hole to hold its flight,
For wormholes twist, and that's not right.
The paper danced, it ran away,
With planets giggling in the Milky Way.

So join me now, let's write and laugh,
At comet trails and a cosmic path.
A sprinkle of humor, a twist of fate,
Let's pen the cosmos, it'll be great!

Celestial Cartography in Verse

With a pencil sharp, I map the skies,
Drawing planets with googly eyes.
Each star is a dot, each comet a line,
Stumbling on orbits that twist and entwine.

A crab-shaped nebula winks with glee,
I really must sketch its bright, funny spree.
While Saturn laughs with its ringed embrace,
Tickling the moons in a playful race.

My chart keeps changing, galaxies swirl,
As comets blow kisses and planets twirl.
But lost in the laughter, I trip, I roll,
In this vast cosmos, humor's the goal.

So throw out the map, let's just explore,
With giggles that echo forevermore.
In this heavenly dance, we find our way,
Through ridiculous routes and cosmic play!

Rhymes for the Reluctant Traveler

A timid traveler at my door,
Said, "I'd rather not explore!"
I laughed and tossed him a shiny key,
"Unlock the universe, come fly with me!"

With sandwich snacks and a trip to Mars,
I promised he'd dance with purple stars.
"Why risk it all?" he asked, all shy,
"Because missing out? That's the real goodbye!"

We hopped on ships that shimmer and glide,
Through asteroid belts with nothing to hide.
His face turned bright, his fears took flight,
As we spun in circles, oh what a sight!

So pack your dreams, forget the doubt,
In this wild journey, we'll laugh it out!
Embrace the odd, the silly, the fun,
In the vastness of space, we've already won!

Free Verse in Zero Gravity

Floating along with snacks in tow,
The universe has no dress code, you know.
My sandwich dances, joyfully spins,
As stars giggle at my comical grins.

Quarks and quasars play peek-a-boo,
In the vacuum, nothing does construe.
Gravity's just a pesky rumor, it seems,
While I munch on cosmic ice cream dreams.

I wear my socks mismatched, quite bold,
Galactic style that never gets old.
Asteroids wink, they find me amusing,
In this vastness, fun is the choosing!

With laughter echoing through the void,
I find that travel's not just enjoyed.
In a world where nothing is quite as it seems,
Every journey is special, no matter the themes.

Starlit Navigations

My compass points to where the laughter flows,
Into the black where mischief grows.
Charting the paths with ukeleles in hand,
Dancing on ether, it's totally unplanned.

Comets leave trails of taffy and cheer,
As aliens party, sipping fizzy beer.
Navigating with giggles, a map made of fun,
Finding new worlds under three moons, just one.

If space had a DJ spinning the tunes,
Satellites would shake their robotic boons.
Around the nebula, I do a jig,
Laughing with planets, doing a big whig!

Across the cosmos, I sail on a whim,
Galaxy games where the lights dim.
Fueled by laughter, I fly through the night,
What a wild ride, no need for a flight.

Rhythms of the Cosmic Traveler

Bounce on stardust, skip through the rays,
Where planets play hopscotch all day.
Each pulsar giggles, a cosmic drum,
Keeping time with a whole lot of fun.

I twist and turn through the milky way,
Finding strange beings who just want to play.
With every encounter, there's laughter anew,
In this astral realm, joy shines like dew.

Lightyears whizz by, what a glorious show,
Chasing laughter where no shadows grow.
With rhythms of friendship leading the way,
I dance through the cosmos, come what may.

Stars wink knowingly, sharing a jest,
In this universe, we are all guests.
Dancing on beams of shimmering light,
The rhythm of travel is purely delight!

Excerpts from an Astral Diary

Day one, I soared on a comet's tail,
Writing with stardust, hoping it won't fail.
Met a blue giant who offered me tea,
Sipped on the universe, feeling so free.

Day four, I got lost in a black hole's grin,
Discovered a zone where chaos begins.
With a wink and a nod, they invited me in,
To play cosmic poker, bets made with spins.

Day seven, I danced on a ring of ice,
Fell into laughter, oh, wasn't it nice!
These moons have humor, a quirky delight,
Spinning their tales under starlit night.

Day ten, I found wisdom from wise old moons,
They said, "Keep your heart, laugh like balloons."
Notes of adventure, penned with a spark,
In this diary of stars, I proudly embark.

Poetic Portals to Other Realms

In a galaxy of giggles and glee,
Portals open, come jump with me.
A comet's tail is a joke unfurled,
Tickling stardust in a wondrous world.

Wormholes waltz with a silly face,
Riding meteors at a frenzied pace.
Each lyric echoes through space-time bends,
Where laughter and verse become good friends.

Nebulae burst with cheerful spree,
Aliens dance on banana trees.
Gravity drops like a clumsy clown,
As we slide through the cosmos upside down.

So grab your pen and a cosmic beam,
In this wild galaxy, we dream our dream.
With rhymes that sparkle and giggles that glow,
To other realms, let the laughter flow.

The Journey Beyond the Stars

Rocket ships made of candy canes,
Zooming through hope, where laughter reigns.
Planets giggle in a wacky conga,
While shooting stars sing a funny saga.

Navigating paths through ticklish haze,
Where black holes burp in cosmic ways.
Each star a friend with a laugh to lend,
On this joyride, no need to pretend.

Asteroids throw jokes at a meteoric speed,
Each punchline a sparkle, a galactic bead.
Through space, we travel with grins and cheer,
In this universe, there's no room for fear.

So pack some giggles and cosmic dreams,
Join this journey, or so it seems.
Beyond the stars, let silly dreams dart,
For laughter's the way to conquer the heart.

Metaphors for the Cosmic Drifter

A cosmic drifter with socks mismatched,
Chasing rainbows, so brightly hatched.
With each lightyear, a chuckle exchanged,
In the tapestry of space, humor's arranged.

Galaxies grin, twinkling in jest,
While time bends like a silly quest.
Comets play tag, with a wink and a cheer,
As the drifter giggles through the void sheer.

Quasars beam laughter, a radiant show,
In the tapestry of stars, the funny winds blow.
With every pun a spark in the dark,
Mosquitoes in space, here comes a quirk!

So join the laughter, step into the light,
A cosmic drifter, soaring in flight.
In the logic of humor, we endlessly wind,
A universe wild, where joy is entwined.

Limericks from the Edge of the Universe

There once was a star with a grin,
Who gathered up friends for a spin.
On the edge of the night,
With laughter so bright,
They danced until dawn's light came in.

A comet slipped on a banana peel,
With a whoosh, oh what a surreal feel!
It twirled through the skies,
With glimmering eyes,
Causing giggles in every big wheel.

An alien cried out, full of glee,
"Let's tickle the moons, just you and me!"
With each swish and swoop,
They made a grand loop,
In a galaxy bursting with glee.

So here at the universe's end,
A limerick's laugh we will send.
With joy as our guide,
On this wild cosmic ride,
Forever, dear friends, we extend.

The Life of a Stardust Nomad

In a ship made of dreams, I roam the skies,
Chasing comets and tales, oh what a prize!
With a towel for a cape, I dance with glee,
Sipping space tea by the light of a starry spree.

Planets twirl like dancers on a cosmic floor,
I wave to Martians, who beg for more.
Moon cheese and laughter fill the interstellar breeze,
What's more absurd? Finding space squirrels with keys.

With every hitch on this galactic ride,
You'll find a friend, it's a joy-filled guide.
We navigate quirks, with delightful grace,
From asteroid bars to the black hole's embrace.

So join me, dear friend, on this wobbling quest,
We'll spin through dimensions, it's truly the best!
In the life of a nomad, there's no room for fear,
Just the love of the stars and a pint of beer.

Sonnets for the Wandering Soul

Oh, the paths of space twist and weave,
I wander through galaxies, would you believe?
Holding onto myths like a cosmic glitch,
Trading my heart for a glow-in-the-dark pitch.

Each leap is a giggle, a bounce in the void,
Where gravity's playful and joy is enjoyed.
The sun winks and nudges; what a cheeky cheer,
While black holes giggle, 'Come closer, my dear!'

The stars hold secrets, but laugh in delight,
As I scribble verses in the soft, velvet night.
With wormholes as rooms in this galactic inn,
I'll toast to the cosmos; let the chaos begin!

So raise your glass high, let your spirit swirl,
In a dance with the universe, give it a twirl.
For wandering souls find their laughter anew,
In the poems we write, the stars' rendezvous.

Verses from the Infinite Road

Just a thumb raised high on the cosmic lane,
I hitch rides on beams, it's a wild terrain.
Robots and aliens, they stop with a smile,
Share tales of the universe, each more worthwhile.

With meteor showers as my speeding lanes,
I giggle through space, ignoring the chains.
The travel bugs nibble on stardust delight,
As I dodge flying sausages in mid-flight.

Oh, journey of nonsense, filled with such charm,
Where bizarre is the norm and fun's the alarm.
From quasars to galaxies, the laughter flows,
On this infinite road, anything goes!

Let's script our adventures in neon hues,
With a wink from the cosmos, we've nothing to lose.
For with every hitch, a new friend appears,
And we dance in the starlight, laughing through years.

Celestial Echoes of the Heart

In a rhythm of galaxies, my heart does play,
As echoes of laughter carry me away.
With meteors as maracas, stars clapping bright,
I party with shadows in the soft, starry night.

The moon lends his light for our spirited dance,
While planets join in, ready to prance.
A symphony of giggles spins through the space,
Where silliness twirls in a cosmic embrace.

So gather your quirks, let the cosmos unfold,
For adventures like these are stories of old.
With a twinkle and wink, the universe sings,
Of stardust and dreams and the joy that life brings.

So let's ride the echoes, with hearts held so dear,
In the laughter of starlight, we have nothing to fear.
For in this vast cosmos, together we dart,
Creating a legacy, celestial echoes of the heart.

Reflections on a Galactic Journey

In search of stars with iced tea in hand,
I waved at comets, they waved back and planned.
Through wormholes and time, I zipped with a grin,
Eating space snacks, let the fun begin!

Aliens danced with their six wiggly legs,
While I taught them how to say 'eggs.'
They showed me a dance I could hardly follow,
But I spun with glee, feeling light as a hollow!

We laughed through the void, our voices a cheer,
As black holes swallowed light, we had no fear.
Every galaxy spun tales full of charm,
In this cosmic playground, nothing could harm!

So here's to the trip, with delight and a spark,
Where laughter echoes through the celestial park.
I'll carry these memories, beyond space's door,
In my heart, they'll shine forevermore!

The Poetry of Parallel Worlds

In a world where socks never match,
I scribbled verses with a detached scratch.
Planets in pajamas played hopscotch with glee,
While time-traveling ducks sip tea with me!

I met my twin, a version so odd,
He painted rainbows with a cosmic rod.
We argued on which way the universe bends,
As gravity giggled and totally pretends.

Across dimensions, each word takes flight,
In realms where the sun can shine at night.
I scribbled my thoughts on a quantum board,
As creatures of whimsy both laughed and soared.

So toast to all worlds, strange and absurd,
Where every odd sentence is wonderfully heard.
In the chaos of space, our minds intertwine,
Creating a poem, both silly and divine!

Saying Goodbye to the Blue Planet

Packing my bags with a smile on my face,
I bid farewell to this lovely old place.
While beaches may miss my sunburnt feet,
I'm off to explore where the space roads meet!

The trees will all wave, their branches a tease,
As I launch in a ship fueled by giggles and cheese.
Earth's sunsets are lovely, but I'll not stay,
For cosmic adventures are just a launch away!

I waved to the oceans, "Don't pout, my dear,"
The stars whispered back, "Come join us here!"
Galaxies beckon with their shimmering lights,
I'm off to the cosmos, on whimsical flights!

So here's to the planet that cradled my youth,
I'll treasure its beauty, and that's the truth.
But space is my ticket, my laughter's my guide,
With dreams on my ship, I'll happily glide!

The Eloquent Silence of Space

In the hush of the void, I hear silence sing,
As stars twinkle softly, like mischievous things.
Planets spin tales with a whispering glance,
While galaxies twirl in an infinite dance!

A quasar giggles at physics' great laws,
While meteors laugh with their shooting star applause.
Comets play dodgeball, with no one to see,
In the stillness of night, they're wild and free!

The echo of nothingness fills me with cheer,
As I drift through the cosmos, my worries unclear.
In the vastness of space, I find a new pace,
Where silence is loud, in this endless embrace.

So let's raise our glasses to the stillness up high,
Where silence speaks volumes, and stardust can fly.
In the heart of the void, I find laughter and grace,
In the eloquent silence of infinite space!

Written on the Winds of the Cosmos

In the quiet space where stars collide,
A senseless whale rides a cosmic tide.
It hums a tune from an alien shore,
While planets laugh and the comets snore.

Floating tea cups in a meteor shower,
Dance to the beat of time's quirky power.
A duck with a hat sits upon a moon,
Sipping stardust and singing a tune.

Swirling thoughts in the vast blue void,
The universe giggles, oh so overjoyed.
A rubber chicken flaps its wings with glee,
As it chases asteroids, oh, what a spree!

Laughing nebulae craft tales in the night,
With cosmic puns that are out of sight.
So if you see a shooting star fly,
Wave to the cosmos, and laugh, oh my!

Sigils of the Swirling Galaxy

A spaceship shaped like a giant shoe,
Zooms past a snail that just painted the blue.
With sigils that sparkle on its bright side,
It leaves behind trails that giggle and glide.

Within the cluster of swirling stars,
A band of squirrels jamming on guitars.
They strum the chords of the cosmic tune,
While asteroids join in, forming a boon.

Aliens argue about the best snacks,
While chasing each other in solar tracks.
One claims that donuts are better than fries,
While another just flings a pie to the skies.

Galactic gossip travels swift and light,
As quarks tell tales that are pure delight.
In the width of the cosmos, let laughter unfurl,
For the fabric of space weaves a whimsical swirl!

Unwritten Chronicles of the Universe

In the corner of space, secrets hang tight,
Whispering tales of a jellybean knight.
With a sword made of marshmallow, bold and brave,
He battles the boredom that galaxies save.

The unwritten stories of planets so shy,
Hide in the craters where stars like to fly.
A belly of laughter, an echoing quack,
As meteors chase a confused little raccoon back.

Wormholes that giggle with stories untold,
Twist time into ribbons, in colors so bold.
A swirling vortex of cosmic jest,
Unfolding the humor, like it's a test.

So raise a glass filled with stardust and cheer,
To wild adventures that bring us near.
In the chronicles unwritten, let joy hold sway,
As humor spins worlds in a brilliant ballet!

Dances of Light in a Vast Expanse

Under the glow of a glittering night,
A disco ball twirls, throwing beams of light.
Planets waltz in a phosphorescent trance,
While asteroids join in a cosmic dance.

Beams of laughter bounce off the moons,
As comets cha-cha to interstellar tunes.
With lightsabers twinkling in black velvet skies,
They duel for the title of best space surprise.

Nebulas swirl in a colorful spree,
Painting laughter on the fabric of glee.
A giant blue octopus waves from afar,
Winking at stardust and wishing on stars.

So join the ballet of the evening light,
Where everything's funny and all feels right.
In the vast expanse of the twinkling night,
Let's dance 'til we burst into laughter's delight!

Hitching a Ride with Words

In a galaxy far, quite bizarre,
Words jump like stars, driving a car.
They zigzag and dance in a brilliant breeze,
Making nonsense rhyme with incredible ease.

A thesaurus begs, 'Please don't misquote!'
While verbs wear hats, and adjectives float.
With puns that flip like pancakes on plates,
Every laugh ignites through cosmic gates.

Consonants cluster like bugs on a seat,
As vowels sing sweetly, a jazzy retreat.
On this road trip of quips, we can't be late,
For humor's the fuel; it drives us straight.

So buckle up tightly, let's giggle and glide,
With hyphens and larks all taking a ride.
In this space where the silly outshines the wise,
We'll hitch a ride under twinkling skies.

Wandering Words of the Universe

Words float on comets in the night sky,
Spinning tales in the silence, oh my!
Puns hitch a lift on stardust trails,
While laughter spills out from echoing sails.

Riddles in orbit, they circle and dive,
Tickling the cosmos, making it thrive.
Galactic giggles in every dark nook,
With punchlines tucked in every good book.

Adventures await in the sighs of the stars,
Where humor and wit chase cosmic bazaars.
Casting shadows of jokes on the moon's bright face,
We ride on whims, exploring this space.

So let's paint this universe with laughter and hue,
With words as our compass, we'll dance as we do.
In this wild, witty wonderland, we explore,
Wandering words that leave us wanting more.

Verses in Interstellar Limbo

In limbo, where verses twist and bend,
Time's a rubber band that doesn't quite end.
Jokes hop through black holes on laughter's beam,
While cosmic giggles create a dream team.

Words weep with joy, floating up like a kite,
In the flux of the void, they shine ever bright.
Metaphors tangle in a dance with a star,
Jesting and jiving, they riff from afar.

Rhymes loop-de-loop in an orbiting spin,
Making sense of nonsense, let the fun begin!
With every quip, we transcend and we soar,
In this interstellar limbo, never a bore.

So grab your space pen and join in the play,
We're scribbling stardust at the end of the day.
In this void of laughter, let your worries fade,
Verses swirl in the starlight, happily made.

Traveling Through the Infinite

Through dimensions we travel with quirky delight,
Words bounce like planets in rhythmic flight.
Galactic giggles paint the stretch of the road,
On a spaceship of humor, lightening the load.

With every swift quip, we unravel the dark,
As comets of laughter ignite a bright spark.
Witty as meteors, we blaze through the night,
Finding joy in the journey, what a splendid sight!

So pack your imagination, let's take off and glide,
In each starlit letter, let's take a wild ride.
Words become fireworks that crash and ignite,
Traveling through the infinite, sheer delight!

Together we'll wander where giggles ascend,
In this cosmic ballet, where no path has an end.
The universe chuckles, and we join with a grin,
Traveling through realms where the fun will begin.

www.ingramcontent.com/pod-product-compliance
Lightning Source LLC
Chambersburg PA
CBHW071848160426
43209CB00003B/460